PRAYER NATIONS

PRAYER NATIONS

When God Suddenly Comes In

DR. KEVIN AND KATHI ZADAI

Unless otherwise indicated, Scripture quotations are taken from the New King James Version. Copyright © 1982 by Thomas Nelson, Inc. Used by permission. All rights reserved.

All Scripture quotations marked (KJV) are taken from the King James Version. Public Domain.

Scripture quotations marked (NLT) are taken from the Holy Bible, New Living Translation, copyright ©1996, 2004, 2015 by Tyndale House Foundation. Used by permission of Tyndale House Publishers, a Division of Tyndale House Ministries, Carol Stream, Illinois 60188. All rights reserved.

Please note that Warrior Notes publishing style capitalizes certain pronouns in Scripture that refer to the Father, Son, and Holy Spirit, which may differ from some publishers' styles. Take note that the name "satan" and related names are not capitalized. We choose not to acknowledge him, even to the point of violating accepted grammatical rules. All emphasis within Scripture quotations is the author's own.

Cover design: Virtually Possible Designs
Editing by Lisa Thompson at www.writebylisa.com
For more information about our school, go to
www.warriornotesschool.com. Reach us on the internet:
www.Kevinzadai.com

ISBN 13 TP: 978-1-6631-0003-0

Dedication

We dedicate this book to the Lord Jesus Christ. When Kevin died during surgery and met with Jesus on the other side, He insisted that Kevin return to life on the earth and help people with their destinies. Because of Jesus's love and concern for people, the Lord has actually chosen to send a person back from death to help everyone who will receive that help so that his or her destiny and purpose is secure in Him.

We want You, Lord, to know that when You come to take us to be with You someday, we sincerely hope that people do not remember us but the revelation of Jesus Christ that You have revealed through us. We want others to know that we are merely being obedient to Your heavenly calling and mission, which is to reveal Your plan for the fulfillment of the divine destiny for each of God's children.

Acknowledgments

In addition to sharing my story with everyone through the book *Heavenly Visitation: A Guide to the Supernatural,* I have been commissioned by God to write over fifty books and study guides thus far. Most recently, the Lord gave me the commission to release this work with my wife Kathi called *Prayer Nations.* This book tells an amazing story of God's faithfulness.

Kathi and I want to thank everyone who has encouraged, assisted, and prayed for us during the writing of this work, especially our spiritual parents Dr. Jesse Duplantis and Dr. Cathy Duplantis. Special thanks to my wonderful wife Kathi for her love and dedication to the Lord and me. Thank you to a great staff for the wonderful job of editing this book. Special thanks as well to all my friends who know about *Prayer Nations* and how to operate in prayer for the next move of God's Spirit!

CONTENTS

Introduction

Kathi and I love the way that God led us to meet each other and chose us to marry and eventually minister to the nations together. We relay many intimate details to you in our new book, *Prayer Nations*. In this book, Kathi shares some intimate details about her life and how God was able to develop her character to become part of this mighty move of God through Warrior Notes. We share some key points, such as "The Plan Is Not Too Grand," "Going the Second Mile," "Get Your Eyes Off Man," "Prayer Nations," "Your Vision from God," "The Fire of God," "The Importance of Words," "Revelation of the Kingdom," "It's God's Plan That Stands," "Rest and Trust in Him," and "God's Original Purpose." We believe that Kathi's insight and wisdom will help you to excel in your journey of pleasing Him in everything you do. Enjoy the book!

Blessings,

Dr. Kevin and Kathi Zadai

PRAYER NATIONS

1

Embers at Dawn

*Most assuredly, I say to you, unless a grain of
wheat falls into the ground and dies, it remains
alone; but if it dies, it produces much grain.*
—John 12:24

*R*ight before I met my husband Kevin, I went
through a death process where I felt like my flame
was going out. In a death process, you typically want
to run away, but when you go through it, life can
come forth. I can best explain the process I went
through by describing a painting we have in our
home.

The painting is a scene of a mountain with a beautiful
campfire at dawn. The fire might have been blazing
the night before, but what is left now are glowing red
embers. God spoke to me about the *Embers at Dawn*
and tied in how the painting represents a death
process, where you think your flame is going out, but
then you survive.

3

In this process of dying, every word that the Lord is speaking to you appears to have died as well. You're living with the Word of God, yet the circumstances around you seem to say exactly the opposite. As John 12:24 says, "Unless a seed falls to the ground and dies, it abides alone; if it dies, it produces much fruit" (my paraphrase). We want to run from the death process, but it helps us and is necessary if we are going to experience life.

The darkest hour is right before the dawn, and if you've ever experienced that, for some reason, it gets extra dark right before morning, right before the birds start singing, and right before a little bit of light peaks over the horizon. Sometimes it even gets colder at that hour. In that moment, the Spirit of the Lord began to blow on me, and the words I had warred over began to flame. I wanted to let go, but I couldn't unless I was willing to let go of the Lord. And I didn't want to do that. You never want to let go of Him.

Regarding the life of Joseph, Psalm 105:19 says, "Until the time that his word came to pass, the word of the Lord tested him." The moment I realized I had survived was when I knew I needed to regain some momentum. The Word of God is incorruptible (1

Peter 1:23), and the Word of God is Jesus. If He has spoken a word to you or over you, that word will stand the test of time and the test of persecution. He is asking you not to let go. If you feel like everything has died, then rejoice and count it as joy. The Bible says for us to count those things as joy when we go through hard times because that which is of God will endure (James 1:2). The plan He has is so much greater than you can see, and there is no limit to what God can do.

The Spirit is saying,

"The Spirit of the Lord is willing to take you to a place of resurrection and ignite all that has seemed to have died. 'Do not delay appearing before Me,' says the Lord, 'for it is time to reconcile all and be healed by my Holy Son Jesus.'"

~Kevin Zadai

PRAYER:
Father, help our friends to trust You in their process of growth. Give them strength and guidance today, Lord. We pray that they would look to You and

nowhere else for their strength. Father, help them trust in You and rely on Your love and protection, no matter what they face. Fan the flame and revive the fire in them, Father. You are in their midst, and they can count it all joy when hardships come. They will endure. We declare that they are victorious and they rise above. Heal their hearts and breathe life on them. In Jesus's name. Amen.

What did the Holy Spirit reveal to you regarding this chapter?

_____

_____

_____

_____

_____

_____

_____

_____

_____

_____

_____

_____

2

The Plan Is Not Too Grand

And do not be conformed to this world, but be
transformed by the renewing of your mind,
that you may prove what is that good and
acceptable and perfect will of God.
—Romans 12:2

God spoke to me and showed me the plan He had for me. At that moment, it seemed so grandiose, as if there were no way it could ever come to pass. At the time, I felt so vulnerable, like a ping-pong ball out in the ocean, so the word He spoke to me seemed far out of reach.

The plan of God surprises you because it's always bigger than what you may have thought. I've learned not to limit God. I've also learned about deception and that you can get out of God's perfect plan through a lack of knowledge. There is a good, perfect, and acceptable plan, and you can settle if you don't have enough revelation (Romans 12:2). That is why Warrior Notes is so big on prayer and worship, and we align ourselves with pure ministries to hear clearly and stay on track.

After the death process, I came to the Lord, and we spent some time together. I asked Him, "Are you mad at me?" I had made an uneducated decision and got into a situation that was not His perfect will for me. He said He was not mad at me, but He knew how much it would hurt, so He was sad that I was hurt. During this time with the Lord, He also spoke to me and said, "The Plan Is Not Too Grand." He meant, "It's not too big. Get out of your head and just believe me." He just wanted me to trust Him.

When He gave me this word, it was my first baby step in the right direction. In this way, He got me focused on moving forward again. From there, the Lord started bringing people into my life who had overcome more difficult situations than I had experienced. To show me how dedicated He was to the word He had given me, the Lord brought a family to me that I ended up living with. I thought, *How did they survive what they went through*? It allowed me to see the victory and imprinted on me that "The Plan Was Not Too Grand." He continued to reinforce the word in me through this family, and I became restored.

I was once coming back from taking care of some legal matters, and my girlfriend Anne, who sees in very black-and-white terms, looked over at me in the car and said, "Katherine, the Lord wants me to tell you that the good that He has for you is so good that you won't remember the bad."

I was thinking, *Well, Anne, that's a nice thought.* I don't know that it penetrated through me at the time because I was so traumatized by what I had gone through.

I had found out that the person I was married to at the time reneged on their covenant. I had to deal with the fact that this person decided that he wasn't going to serve God even if it was God's will. He was going to go back into his former lifestyle, which would bring judgment on him. Marriage is a covenant, but God gives people free will to choose, and you can't follow a person into sin. It was very tearing, but God spoke to me and said, "I have some good things coming for you, and it's going to work out." That word was like a light in the darkness, providing a ray of hope.

As a young Christian, I thought that everyone encountered the same born-again experience. When I was born again, I was delivered of so much that it was like night and day. I came into school one day, and one of the girls in the lunchroom said, "I heard you got baptized last night." They were all wondering, *What happened to Kathi?*

I thought that this was how it was with everyone who came to know Jesus. When I dealt with what I did with the person I was married to, I thought that we were fine since they were born again also. I assumed that he had as miraculous of deliverance as I did and that there would be no problems. Then I learned that because of free will, people process events differently.

The Lord reminded me of the verse, "Owe no man anything but to love one another" (Romans 13:8). He told me not to focus on this person but to judge myself and remain clean to come out of the situation. A scripture that supports this says, "You will not get out until you have paid the last penny" (Matthew 5:26).

The Lord continued to reach out to him not to restore our marriage but to restore his eternal relationship with God. He just kept returning to his old lifestyle, and there was no repentance. The Lord began to speak to me about divorce, and I didn't want that. I came from a family of divorce, and that was not on my radar. For me, it would be the worst thing to have to go through. It would be the ultimate feeling of abandonment and rejection.

One day, I was in a church service, and the word of the Lord came to me. I had been in possession of the divorce papers for several months, but I couldn't bring myself to move forward. The Lord said, "This is the day. Get out and don't ever look back. I will carry you as a Shepherd would carry a lamb. I'll carry you all the days of your life." In this prophecy, He spoke to me about my restoration and about Kevin. It was a beautiful prophecy. He spoke about the ministry and how the Lord would use me. The *rhema* word for me at that moment was to "get out and don't look back." [1]

There is pure prophecy, and this was undoubtedly the word of the Lord for me, and I was activated by it. Anytime you receive a word, it is wise to judge the prophecy. I had the knowledge of what I was supposed to do, but once that word of the Lord came to me and I was activated by it, I never looked back. I knew that not divorcing this individual would mean that I would be endorsing what he was doing. The

---

[1] "Strong's #4487: rhema," Bible Tools, accessed October 11, 2021,
https://www.bibletools.org/index.cfm/fuseaction/Lexicon.sho
w/ID/G4487/rhema.htm.

Lord gave him space for repentance, but he didn't choose it, and I knew then that if I didn't get out, I would become part of the problem. He was in a lifestyle where he was unfaithful to the covenant and cheating, which was grounds for divorce.

My pastor paid for the divorce once he saw that I was moving forward with it. I believe it was the Lord helping me even though I didn't need that; it was like a token of His love toward me. Afterward, I realized I was in the Lord's hands, and I began to have rapid restoration. I started receiving the new vision where the old one had died, and I entered a place of rest. I began relying on the Lord for His direction.

The Spirit is saying,

"I want to take you to where you have never been. My plan is bigger than what you can handle on your own so that all will know that I am your God and I am doing this profound thing. Your borders are about to expand."

~Kevin Zadai

PRAYER:

We pray for the hearts of our friends and partners who are reading this. We pray for restoration and revelation. Father, give them Your plan so that they may walk in the fullness of it. Father, put hope in them to continue the race. There is nothing that You can't do. Lord, put the right people in their lives to come alongside them in their journey. We declare for Your peace to come and rest on them, that they'll no longer strive to do things in their own strength but that they'll seek You to provide the next steps. In Jesus's name. Amen.

What did the Holy Spirit reveal to you regarding this chapter?

_____

_____

_____

_____

_____

_____

_____

_____

_____

3

Going the Second Mile

Now faith is the substance of things hoped for,
the evidence of things not seen.
—Hebrews 11:1 KJV

I found out that we go through a process,
which doesn't happen in an instant. It's one thing to
say, "I'm going to serve and obey God," but it's
another thing to stick with it and go the second mile.
It's as though you're a runner in a long-distance race.

When I was on the mission field in Micronesia, I was
tested to go the second mile. I ended up serving two
terms in total, but before the second term was up, I
didn't want to be there anymore. The first time I
went, I was so excited. After that, I went back again
almost a year later, and it was tough because I knew
I was supposed to be there. When I found out I was
going back for a second term, I was excited at first.
My mom drove me to the airport, and we were both

crying because we didn't know when I would return. I had felt called to stay there forever.

I went with a ministry called "Youth with a Mission" (YWAM). The first part of the program is a practical portion of the discipleship training school. You spend the first half, about two or three months, on the base, getting to know God. The other half is outreach where you make Him known. Everyone worked and went to classes. We had put together a play that preached the Gospel for the outreach portion, and you could understand it without words. We had also delivered the play with narration in several other languages.

I had just completed my practical classes and was about to start the outreach portion of the program, and I wanted to leave. I called my mom, convinced it was time to come home. I said, "Mom, I need a ticket so I can come back to the States."

She said, "Honey, you know I can't do that. You need to stay." Yet another voice was telling me, nudging me, and putting their foot down to go the second mile. My mom had a mercy gift, and she loved me, so for her to say no and tell me I could not come home would have been very hard to do.

So I stayed. We were flying to the outer islands where the outreach was going to be, and the Lord broke my heart in a powerful way. The area we flew into had electricity, but the remote outer islands we were going to did not. Suddenly, as we came into this remote area without electricity, I heard the Lord say, "The poor and needy search for water, but there is none, but I, the Lord their God will hear from heaven and heal their land." Instantly, I felt His compassion. I knew how much He loved me, yet He allowed me to be uncomfortable to reach them. People's lives were changed, especially a gentleman by the name of Lazarus. He came back to the Lord. He had found out about Jesus when he was in California at college and had difficulty returning to the islands. When our team went there, he felt as if we had come especially for him, and perhaps we had.

After I returned from the mission field, I knew I was stepping into a season of my life where I would be married. I had prayed about it, but when I got back, it was the first time I ever had that knowledge, and I received the revelation that I was in a new season. I could feel the shift, and so I found someone who fit my qualifications. I thought, *This is probably it,* even though now, in hindsight, this person wasn't my heart's desire. It was more as if I had settled.

After that relationship fell through and I was healing from it, I was sitting on a dock in Washington State. I was spending time with the Lord and began to read Hebrews 11:1. I've read that verse often and knew it well, but this time, the words just dropped into me, and suddenly, my faith was evident. I knew I would be restored in the area of marriage.

Sometimes we don't like the season of life we're in, but if we could just hold onto the word that we are contending for, we will see the fruit of it. Mark 4:17 says, "Persecution arises for the word's sake," so we can't take it personally. It's part of the bigger picture. Hold onto the words you've been given, and they will become part of you. Once you reach the other side of the word that's being challenged, you can impart that word to other people who are willing to receive it. I knew one thing: I would be restored in the area of marriage. It was so real to me, and I knew it.

I continued living with the family, who were my pastors, and one night I came home from a Bible study. I was feeling so positive about everything that I said, "I think I'm ready to move out and get an apartment with one of the girls at church."

Their response was, "Well, Miss Kathi, we feel like you should really see this out till the end and stay here with us." I respected them and agreed, but I felt as if I were ready to move on.

In this situation, going the second mile meant that I had submitted to them and what they were seeing for me. They saw the restoration that was coming. They had already seen Kevin in the Spirit, and a short time later, he received the word to come to our church. The Lord was working, and it paid off because I was in the right place at the right time. You want to be *went* not *sent*. You want the situation to be so positive that you don't want to leave, but then it's time. It's a principle, and like Jesus said, "No man takes my life, but I lay it down" (John 10:18). Ensure the ball is in your court before you decide, and don't act under pressure. Go the second mile. Make sure that you are in such a great place that you don't want to leave. Then leave.

The Spirit is saying,

"I have seen your commitment to Me and My purpose, and I will reward you. Do not hesitate to walk with Me further because your character is so important for what I have for you. Don't allow circumstances to discourage you, for I have your reward in My hand."

~Kevin Zadai

PRAYER:

Lord, we pray today that You would give strength and courage to the people to stick it out and go the second mile. When it seems like they should move forward, Father, provide them with wisdom because what You have in store is greater than they can see. Let them know what Your good, acceptable, and perfect will for them is. Father, we pray that they would seek You and that You would open their ears to hear and their eyes to see what You have in store. In Jesus's name, Amen.

What did the Holy Spirit reveal to you regarding this chapter?

_____

_____

_____

_____

_____

_____

_____

_____

_____

_____

_____

_____

_____

_____

_____

_____

_____

4

Get Your Eyes Off Man

The fear of man brings a snare, But whoever
trusts in the Lord shall be safe.
—Proverbs 29:25

The Lord spoke to me. "Get your eyes off man. I have not forgotten you." Before He spoke that word, I hadn't realized my eyes were on man, so I began to examine myself. We want to pay attention to what's motivating us. When you have the fear of the Lord, then you are aware of your motives because you want to make sure you are acting on God's agenda and not your own. I began to study Proverbs 29:25 to gain more understanding.

To fear God is the beginning of wisdom. It is having a reverence toward God—to serve Him and love Him with all your heart. When we fear Him, it sets our priorities in order. It is the Lord's plan that will stand. When you have the fear of man, then man has power over you, and he can manipulate you in your soul. If I would've listened to the fear of man, I wouldn't be where I am today because I probably would've done what everyone else was telling me to do. I may not have ever gone to the mission field.

I have learned a great deal about the fear of man versus the fear of God, including the day I met Kevin. I was in the church service, and I hadn't met him yet, but the Lord told him where I was. We had a guest minister that day. The presence of God was so strong in that service, and the Lord asked me, "What are you going to do about what I promised you?" I knew that the Lord was referring to being restored in the area of marriage.

I was shocked that He had asked me that question. I realized that I had become so focused on other aspects that I was no longer fully trusting Him in that area. I had this fixation of ensuring I did everything right to be restored. The church was doing very well; it was on fire, and I was growing like a weed. I had become comfortable in living with the pastors. We were riding, training, and showing horses. It was a restorative time in my life. I was surprised when the Lord asked me what I was going to do about what He had promised me.

I judged myself, and I thought, *I need to get back into faith.* At first, I thought God meant that He wanted me to start believing for my previous husband to come back to the Lord. So I said, "Okay, Lord, I will do that even if my pastors think I'm nuts." They would've because they prayed me through that situation. I said, "Lord, even though they'll think I'm nuts, I will start believing for that person to come back to you, standing for him and praying for him." The Lord used that to uproot the fear of man in me.

Immediately when the service let out, I went to my friend Karen, and I told her, "I made a covenant with the Lord. I'm going to start believing for this person to come back to the Lord again." She nodded. I continued, "All right. I just want to be accountable to you."

As I was telling her about this covenant, a woman of God by the name of Dottie walked up to me and said, "I'd like you to meet my friend." I wasn't looking to meet anyone's friend at that point, but because Dottie was such a sweet and beautiful woman of God, I agreed to meet him. Well, her friend was Kevin.

I was willing to face my pastors' rejection to get right in my heart and get right with God. I was about to make the agreement to start believing for this person again, but the Lord didn't need me to do that; He just needed my faith. The Lord wanted to see my heart. It's similar to Abraham when God asked him to sacrifice Isaac. Because of Abraham's obedience, God could see that he had the fear of the Lord. As a result, God promised him all the blessings (Genesis 22). We can't always see it, but there are many intricacies to God's plan. That's how I got rid of the fear of man.

The Spirit is saying,

"I, the Lord, am the One who has called, you and will confirm to you the path and the ways that I do things. No one can do what I do, and I have bought you. You are mine."

~Kevin Zadai

PRAYER:

Lord, we thank You for Your wisdom and authority that come in the most vulnerable moments of our lives. Lord, You alone are worthy. We pray that our partners and friends would look to Your face and seek You. We pray that they would get their eyes off man and that they would set their faces like flint on

You. Father, increase their faith would rise and may Your power meet them there. I pray that they only say what You are saying and do what You are doing. I pray that they would know that your ways are higher and that faith triumphs over fear. Father, may they know that they have overcome because You overcame. In Jesus's name. Amen.

What did the Holy Spirit reveal to you regarding this chapter?

_____

_____

_____

_____

_____

_____

_____

_____

_____

_____

_____

_____

PRAYER NATIONS

5

Prayer Nations

"Before she was in labor, she gave birth; before her pain came, she delivered a male child. Who has heard such a thing? Who has seen such things? Shall the earth be made to give birth in one day? Or shall a nation be born at once? For as soon as Zion was in labor, she gave birth to her children. Shall I bring to the time of birth, and not cause delivery?" says the Lord. "Shall I who cause delivery shut up the womb?" says your God.
—Isaiah 66:7–9

*C*an a nation be born in one day? The answer is yes, with persistent prayer! Prayer is done by faith, through yielding to the Holy Spirit. Various forms of prayer include speaking the Scriptures and praying in tongues. In the life of a Christian, prayer is consistent and constant throughout your day. It is a natural form of communication with your heavenly Father.

Prayer Nations is the revelation that, *yes, a nation can be born in a day.* Yes, a family can be born in a day. Yes, you can be delivered in a day. Yes, your church can go to the next level in a day!

You pray from the revelation that it can happen in a day. It's the way God operates. Before you call, He answers. While you are yet speaking, He hears. He speaks, and then He sees. It's getting into that flow with God. Otherwise, you have the mentality of believing it when you see it, and that's not God, and it's not faith. You were not created to *believe it when you see it.* You were created to *speak it and then see it.* That's how God created us. The Lord's vision is that He calls things that are not as though they were (Romans 4:17).

Jehovah El Roi means "Jehovah sees."[2] He sees the truth and sees the future. He doesn't need evidence because He is the evidence. However, we are to live by faith and speak from the Spirit. Prayer is not just making requests; prayer is proclaiming, declaring, and standing firm on what God has already said. My heart is that people would get into a place and

---

[2] Hope Bolinger, "Meaning and Importance of God's Name 'El Roi'- The God Who Sees Me," Bible Study Tools, July 21, 2020, https://www.biblestudytools.com/bible-study/topical-studies/reasons-to-praise-god-as-el-roi.html.

position of constant prayer. In Isaiah 45:11, the Lord says, "And concerning the work of My hands, you command Me."

We should be praying, asking, and seeking the Father. That's the type of relationship we're called to, and we need to live there without striving. We waste a lot of energy trying to get to a place we were already called to. It has to do with lukewarmness in the church, and Jesus addresses this in the Bible.

In Revelation, the first few chapters talk about how people fall away, becoming cold or lukewarm, more easily than going toward God and becoming hot. This is because we are in a fallen world and in a constant war. We must remind ourselves of the truth and who we are in Christ because our identity is found in Him.

All people are God's, and He created us all for Himself. "The earth is the Lord's, and all its fullness, The world and those who dwell therein" (Psalm 24:1). *Prayer Nations* is about individuals and groups being nations. Your home is a nation. Warrior Notes is a nation. The purpose is to first be ignited as individuals so that you can take the fire to your church and work and possess the land. A nation can be born in a day. You may not see it in a day physically; however, it can happen in the Spirit, and we are not to grow weary. God says that all men would pray lifting holy hands (1 Timothy 2:8). He wants us all to pray this way, lifting our holy hands and letting the light of God come out of our mouths and hands to change the atmosphere wherever we are.

All prayer comes from a place of rest. When praying in the Spirit, we must enter the rest and yield to the Holy Spirit. Let the Spirit carry you. As I have heard Sister Ruth Carneal say and even as Ruth Heflin has taught, "There is an ease in the glory." It's not done from works but from rest. Do everything you can to enter the rest. The Bible says that we are to labor to enter the rest (Hebrews 4:11); the rest is the promised land. You should be putting energy in your walk with God; you are in covenant with Him, yielding your members to Him, and you will enter this rest. "For with stammering lips and another tongue He will speak to this people, To whom He said, 'This is the rest with which You may cause the weary to rest,' and, 'This is the refreshing,' Yet they would not hear" (Isaiah 28:11–12).

You're most productive when you're acting from resting in the Spirit rather than from striving in the flesh realm. Isaiah prophesies about speaking in tongues, the baptism of the Holy Spirit, and rest and refreshing. Jude 1:20 also says to keep building yourself up on your most holy faith and praying in the Holy Spirit. You use faith to pray in the Spirit because otherwise, it doesn't make sense. You strengthen your faith by praying in tongues.

Don't grow weary in well-doing. You will see the return of your perseverance. You can affect everything around you with the Holy Spirit in you and the Word of God coming out of your mouth. When you have the revelation that it can happen in a day, you realize how effective you are. Every time you pray, you're sowing into the next generation.

Prayer can change the course of history, which is when you know it has become effective. When you pray, pray for what you want to see on earth. Pray for God to have His way. Pray for the purity of the pulpits in this nation. Pray that the Word of God proceeds like fire from the pulpits and that His Word is not bound or hindered. Pray that God works with your pastor, confirming the Word with signs and wonders following. Be a people of prayer, a people who acknowledge Him, who stand in faith together. I want to see people come into agreement in prayer, ready and mobilized for intercession. Be a people that know who they are in Christ, a people who are world changers and history makers!

The Spirit is saying,

"Allow Me to gather you together with the right people so that I can accomplish all that is perfect for My plan for this generation. Love one another and pray for one another. You will see Me in your midst as My glory comes in."

~Kevin Zadai

PRAYER:

Father, we pray that Your children would know the importance of consistent prayer, that when they proclaim a thing, it moves mountains. So that whatever they ask in Your name, it will be done. Increase their faith. Increase their capacity to know that a nation can be born in a day. Open their eyes and their awareness, Lord, that they can affect the whole world because of the Holy Spirit in them. Give them a fire to go into the marketplace and release Your love to people. Stir them up, Lord, to share their testimony of what You've done. Father, You're already in their future, establishing their steps. May they lean not on their own understanding but trust in You and go forward. For You, Lord, are directing their paths. We pray this in the mighty name of Jesus. Amen.

What did the Holy Spirit reveal to you regarding this chapter?

_____

_____

_____

_____

_____

_____

_____

_____

_____

_____

_____

_____

_____

_____

_____

6

Your Vision from God

The earth is the Lord's, and the fulness thereof;
the world, and they that dwell therein.
—Psalm 24:1 KJV

he earth is the Lord's, and all the people are His. Our authority is in Him, and the earth is ours. The world does not belong to the devil; it belongs to the Lord. He gave the earth to Adam and Eve, and then Jesus came back and got a better covenant for us. Once people have revelation from God, they realize how potent and effective they are on earth.

Without a vision or a revelation, the people will cast off restraint (Proverbs 29:18). This is saying that we essentially perish without vision. When Jesus was asking the disciples, "Who do you say that I am?" they all gave different answers, but Peter had the revelation. He said, "Thou art the Christ, son of the living God."

Jesus said, "Blessed are you, for flesh and blood hasn't revealed this to you, but my Father, which is in heaven" (Matthew 16:16–17).

Peter had the revelation given by God to know this. Like Peter, God wants to provide you with revelation into all that He has for you and your life. Revelation and vision come through our prayers and an intimate relationship with the Father. He opens your eyes to the vision He has for you and reveals His intentions. It has to do with walking out the path you're on. He's gone into your future and paved the way for that future (Psalm 139).

Sometimes, when God gives you a vision, He picks a fight. In Samson's case, He was looking for an opportunity to wage war with the Philistines. Before Samson was born, an angel appeared to his mother and told her everything that would happen with Samson (Judges 13:1–5). God always has a reason for what He does. The evidence of that is being fulfilled right now as you step forward.

When we pick a fight, it needs to be as the Word of the Lord is spoken. I do not doubt that God can work through anyone to be healed, delivered, and set free.

The blood of Jesus can go to the deepest depths and save us. That's picking a fight! When moving in the vision God has for you, you must write it out. When we write it out, we can look back and see how God's hand was in it and how great and immeasurable the return was. I wasn't given a word or prophecy to write books, but I saw the importance and how it will accomplish the vision and affect others.

Habakkuk says to write the vision so that he that reads it can run (Habakkuk 2:2). You're writing the vision not just for yourself but for others as well. When anything happens with us, we are affecting the body of Christ, and we can see other people take the vision and run. He uses us to help others in the process. If God hadn't gotten Kevin and me out of debt, we wouldn't be able to help others. God made it possible for us to prosper to be a blessing to others to see them thrive. It began with us writing down our debts and declaring them canceled.

We once attended the Southwest Believer's Convention, and it was supernatural. We had room #777, and our bill was $1111.11. Some powerful things happened in the services as well. We learned about taking authority and walking in it. In one of the sessions, Reverend Jerry Savelle said, "I want everybody in here to write down everything you owe." We didn't write down our house because we didn't think of it at the time, but we wrote down all our credit cards, the car, etc. He said, "I want you to pray over these and say that debt, poverty, and lack are broken." We did this, and I tucked it away in my wallet.

We would pray together in the mornings on our way to work, declaring that debt and lack were broken over our lives. It became part of what we prayed and agreed upon. Years later, it happened. I came across that piece of paper, and I looked at it and said to Kevin, "Honey, look, they're all gone. All the debts are gone." After all the Lord has done, that seems minor now, but this was the beginning, and we said, "If it's happened for other people, it can happen for us."

A short time later, a pastor that we were helping came to our house, and every time he came over, he said, "I see your house paid for." We started writing on our mortgage checks: "Paid in full." We just quoted what our pastor had prophesied over us, and it came to pass. We also had put a little sticker on the door that said "Paid in full." We were determined, and since then, we've had three paid-in-full houses, including the home we live in now. It feels good not to have any bills, but at the time, it seemed impossible. It's not impossible, but you have to start somewhere.

A picture paints a thousand words. That's why I love testimonies because they paint a picture. Once, we were in service, and it was one of the first times we ever went to see Jesse Duplantis. We sowed a seed, and he said, "I want you to write what your seed is going toward." He called it "naming your seed." I drew a house, horses, a car, a dog, household salvation, and an airplane. Over the years, we have seen most of these things come to pass, and we recently got the jet. It's powerful when we write out the vision. My encouragement to you is not to be afraid to dream and write it out. Make sure to include Scriptures to go with your vision. God is not afraid of your vision, and no matter what you dream, what He has is even more significant. It's bigger than you can imagine (Ephesians 3:20).

Seeing the vision, such as a vision board, is a great way to express yourself. We have various Scriptures and paintings hung up in our house that all have specific meaning to them. They either represent breakthroughs we've had or what we are believing God will provide. I have one picture of a Jet SR71 called *Peacekeepers*. I look at that often and pray when God sends us out to different places. It's always great to keep the vision before your eyes. Whether you see yourself being healed, going into ministry, or getting married, put the vision in front of you and proclaim that it is yours. "You shall no longer be termed Forsaken, nor shall your land any more be termed Desolate; But you shall be called Hephzibah, and your land Beulah; for the Lord delights in you, And your land shall be married" (Isaiah 62:4).

Before I met Kevin, the Lord gave me Isaiah 62:4, and later, I came to find that He also gave that passage to Kevin. The Lord told me that I was sought out, so I began proclaiming that my land is married and that I'm the Lord's delight. Not long after that, I met Kevin, so it pays to be in the right church service. It's also essential to write the vision down, make it plain, proclaim it, and enforce it.

Sometimes, what we're praying for does not come to pass, and that could be because we need to make an adjustment or because the timing isn't right. On the other hand, it may have to do with us, or our vision might be too small. We don't always know the details, but we still must believe. "For the vision is yet for an appointed time; But at the end it will speak, and it will not lie. Though it tarries, wait

for it; Because it will surely come, It will not tarry"
(Habakkuk 2:3).

The Spirit is saying,

"Allow me to gather you together with the right people so that I can accomplish all that is perfect for my plan for this generation. Love one another and pray for one another. You will see me in your midst as my glory comes in."

~Kevin Zadai

PRAYER:

Lord, we pray for our friends and partners, that they will write the vision and make it plain. We pray, Father, that You'll provide them with the creativity of the kingdom, that they will know there are no limits to what You can do through them, that what You have is so much bigger than they can see in the natural. Open their spiritual eyes, Father, to the abundance of Your kingdom. Just as when we wrote the vision and sowed seeds toward our future, we saw it come to pass. Do it for them, Father, and we declare that their debts are paid in full, their homes are paid off, and that it is done in Your Name for those believing to be married. Jesus, You are their provider. They don't have to fear because there is no fear in love, and You love them unconditionally. In Jesus's name. Amen.

What did the Holy Spirit reveal to you regarding this chapter?

_____

_____

_____

_____

_____

_____

_____

_____

_____

_____

_____

_____

7

The Fire of God

John answered their questions by saying, "I baptize you with water; but someone is coming soon who is greater than I am—so much greater that I'm not even worthy to be his slave and untie the straps of his sandals. He will baptize you with the Holy Spirit and with fire.
—Luke 3:16 NLT

Embrace the fire of God—do not run from it, yield to it. When we yield to the fire, we receive what it's meant to do. The fire is our friend; God wants us to sit with Him and not run. He is a consuming fire, and that fire will ignite what is of the Lord and burn up what is not of Him. As we surrender ourselves to Him, the refiner's fire purifies and cleanses us because we are so precious to Him.

On the day of Pentecost, when the Holy Spirit came upon them, they weren't just speaking in tongues.

But tongues of fire rested on them. The fire of God on your tongue has a purifying outcome. That's why praying in tongues is so effective. If you want to be a pure vessel for the Lord, praying in other tongues is one way to embrace the fire. As you pray in tongues, the Holy Spirit may bring up concerns that you need to deal with, and when you pray, it's like one thread that unties the big knot. He will help you resolve these matters. When events happen that are contrary to what you desire, don't run; stay in the fire and count it all joy. Let Him purify you.

Lucifer had that fire, but he became defiled, and the fire of God consumed him because iniquity was found in him. As believers, the fire of God is in us and on us. We're allowed to have the fire, and it does not consume us because of God's mercy and the blood of Jesus. It's very humbling to be allowed to have God's fire in our lives. In heaven, the fire is everywhere and is at a heightened level because of purity. Holiness is a standard in heaven. The fire of God wants to consume anything inappropriate, so when the fire begins to move in your life, expect there to be some changes.

We are born again not of corruptible seed but of the incorruptible seed of the Word of God (1 Peter 1:23). Anything that's born of God overcomes the world. If something in your life is born of God, it will overcome. It will survive the fire. It will even grow stronger in the fire, but if it doesn't, it won't, and you don't want it anyway. The fire of God is consuming, and it purifies, and anything in it that shouldn't be there may disappear in a puff of smoke.

Jesus is coming, and we have a lot of homework to do. It's time to pick up the pace and finish the race. One way we can embrace the fire is just by saying yes. Say yes to the Lord, and it will burn up what is not of Him. Mary said, "Yes. Be it unto me according to thy word" (Luke 1:38). That's what we should be saying. In just a simple agreement with the Lord, we become aligned with heaven. When you agree with God's Word and what He's telling you and you come into agreement with heaven, the angels, who are flames of fire, can work with you unhindered.

We are called to be holy and set apart, and God set us apart as holy unto Him. In heaven, the angels are holy angels. The fire is holy fire. Everything in heaven is holy. "Holy, holy, holy, is the Lord God Almighty, who was and is and is to come" (Revelation 4:8). He has given us everything we need for life and godliness. He has given us this fire for a reason.

The Spirit is saying,

"I have created holy fire for you to dwell within on the earth. I have come to you with this fire because I am a consuming fire. Never doubt that I will reward you for walking in My holiness."

~Kevin Zadai

PRAYER:

Father, we pray that Your people will prepare themselves and be ready for the coming of Your Son Jesus. Let their hearts not be troubled. Lord, if they need to repent, lead them to repentance now. Burn up anything that is not of You so that they can come upon the sapphire stone, pure, face-to-face with You without hindrance. Give them strength to rise above and set them in motion. Lord, for those seeking the gift of tongues, baptize them now with tongues of fire. Release in them the fire of God right now. May fire be released in these individuals. Fire. Fire. Fire. Holy fire of God, burn in them. In Jesus's name. Amen.

What did the Holy Spirit reveal to you regarding this chapter?

_____

_____

_____

_____

_____

_____

_____

_____

_____

_____

_____

_____

_____

_____

_____

_____

_____

_____

8

The Importance of Words

*And so blessing and cursing come pouring out of
the same mouth. Surely, my brothers and sisters,
this is not right!*
—James 3:10 NLT

*G*od started everything with words. We were
created in His image, so we do not want any corrupt
communication to come out of our mouths. James
talks about how we do not want good and bad to
come out of the same fountain because life and death
are in the power of your tongue. (See also Proverbs
18:21.) Your words are powerful.

If you can't find the right words to say, you don't
have to say anything. It's hard to win a spiritual battle
in the natural, so you might need to be quiet until you
know what to say. Let the Lord give you the words
and the reply of your tongue. When you speak words
of truth, you will be speaking in the direction you
want to go. Psalm 119:130 says, "The entrance of

Your words gives light." When you are speaking words of truth, you will be helping others see. In your light, we see the light. You are created in God's image, so not speaking the truth in a situation is like a fish trying to breathe air or a human trying to breathe underwater. You were created to speak where you are going.

Even though I was divorced at the time, I would say, "The truth is that I am sought out, I am the Lord's delight, and my land is married." When I was married and had a mortgage, we would say, "We're debt-free." We were calling things that were not as though they were like our Father does. His words do not return void.

When your words are lined up with God and with heaven, a peace comes to you. At that point, the angels are free to help you. The angels love it when we speak life-giving words, but we can grieve them when we speak the opposite of the truth. We do not want to grieve them.

We also have access to the reset button, which is called repentance. If we speak wrong words, we can say, "Lord, I repent of wrong words, deeds, and actions. I repent of doubt and unbelief." Sometimes

I do this as a check-up because I don't want anything in me that opposes the truth. I call it "doing a check-up from the neck up."

Your voice is your address. You may say, "Well, everyone else is singing and saying something," but the reality is that *you* need to sing and use *your* voice. You need to speak because God likes your sound. He made you, and He decided that He wanted you. A song in you needs to come out, and words within you need to be heard not just for you but for the generations after you. You might say, "Well, no one in my family has ever spoken like this," but you could be the first one to turn it around with your words. You can start sowing seeds of truth over your generations. You can speak out and say, "My generations will serve the Lord. They will prosper and walk in good health." When you start speaking where you are going, everything changes.

We saw a shift when we heard the Lord tell us to work extra, and we worked double shifts for ten years. If we hadn't changed how we spoke or lived, we wouldn't have seen a shift. Our priorities began to change, and instead of feeling like victims, we knew we were where God wanted us. Before we met, we were called to ministry and worked ministry jobs, but then we were called to work in secular jobs. I became a cosmetologist, and Kevin went to work as a flight attendant. We would not have chosen these professions on our own, but we knew God had called us to those careers, and it was supernatural. We had a lot of favor at those jobs. There was no striving because we were sent. We began to speak to the Lord, and just as He called us to our jobs, He could call us out.

There is a beginning and an end. We knew we couldn't say we were done at our jobs but that it had to come from Him and by the word of the Lord. You can speak to your destination and say things like, "I hear His voice, and the voice of a stranger I will not follow, and I am more than a conqueror." Your spirit becomes excited when it hears the Word of God, and by this process, your spirit causes God's will to come to pass.

When you pray in tongues and meditate on the Word of God, it becomes part of you. It's as if there's a compass within you. As you speak the Scriptures and pray in tongues, it goes in your ears and registers in your spirit. Then your inner compass begins to line up with those words. Your cells and your mind will be happy when they hear the Word of God. People around you will become blessed by the resurrection life that's on you and in the Word of God.

The Word of God that you're speaking is not just words; it's Jesus, and He conquered hell, death, and the grave! He resurrected and ascended. These are resurrection words. These are words of truth, and our bodies were created to respond to the written and spoken Word of God. It is the holy Word of God, the Holy Bible. God spoke these worlds into existence through His Word. He framed the world with His words. We need to remember that we're speaking from the Spirit. We can call things that are not as though they were. We can say to mountains, "Be removed." If we don't doubt in our hearts but we believe in what we say with our mouths, it's going to be done (Mark 11:23). The same principle that we became born again by works in all areas of our lives.

When we would get a new house or office, Kevin and I would speak out about what we wanted to see. We would call the walls salvation and the gates praise. We used Scriptures and spoke over the buildings that they would be glorified and beautified and reflect Him. We would call those things that were not as though they were until they happened. We've seen them come to pass, and we know that this works because it is the Word of God and how He works.

The Spirit is saying,

"I spoke the worlds into existence from the beginning. I desire that you would enforce what I have spoken by proclaiming the truth about your situation. Call those things that are not as though they are. This proclamation will bring My will into manifestation on your behalf."

~Kevin Zadai

PRAYER

Father, we pray that faith would rise in Your people today. Let them know that they are overcomers by the blood of the Lamb and the word of their testimony. When they speak, let them choose their words wisely. Father, may the Word of God be on their tongues when they speak. Help them remember that Your Word is truth and has power. May they speak in the direction they are going and speak life over themselves and others. Fill them to overflowing so that anyone they come in contact with will encounter You, Father. Let them be the light in the darkness and have the power and authority through You to bring people into your glorious light through Your Son Jesus. I bless them in Jesus's name. Amen.

What did the Holy Spirit reveal to you regarding this chapter?

_____

_____

_____

_____

_____

_____

_____

_____

_____

_____

_____

_____

_____

_____

_____

_____

_____

_____

9

Revelation of the Kingdom

Who hath heard such a thing? Who hath seen
such things? Shall the earth be made to bring
forth in one day? Or shall a nation be born at
once? For as soon as Zion travailed, she
brought forth her children. Shall I bring to the
birth, and not cause to bring forth?
saith the Lord: shall I cause to bring forth
and shut the womb? saith thy God.
—Isaiah 66:8–9 KJV

*P*rayer Nations is not only a revelation but a
kingdom principle. As I said before, "Yes, a nation
can be born in a day," and He can answer before you
call. God's nature is to be in our future; it's how He
works. However, I want you to see something that
takes this a step further: the concept of *travailing*.
This is a feeling that happens in the Spirit like you're
having a baby. We've never had kids, but I have had
horses that have had babies, and I've experienced
travailing in the Spirit.

Can you imagine getting ready to have a baby, but the baby is already there? The Lord wants us to see that before we travail, we've already birthed it. That's how fast it can happen. Before you think you will have to die, you've already been resurrected. Don't give up your ground—stand firm. "If the spirit of the ruler rises against you, do not leave your post; for conciliation pacifies great offenses" (Ecclesiastes 10:4).

Before you travail, you may experience a dark hour. Your circumstances may seem so intense and unbearable at that point, but then you'll experience the breakthrough. There's a tipping point, and just when you think it's not going to happen, that's when it will happen. You may have been believing God for your dreams, and you don't foresee that they will happen. Just when it gets so heavy, suddenly, you receive the breakthrough. Then when the baby comes; it's as if you don't remember the difficulty anymore. When God's restoration comes, you don't remember the bad.

That's why we want to gird up our minds because when we're in a battle, we feel as if we're all alone. We hear the lies like, "God will not come through."

We must remind ourselves that a nation can be born in a day. It's like that word my friend had for me. "The good that God has is so good that you won't remember the bad." When His restoration comes, you will not remember the bad. Before you travail, you're going to bring forth. If you do happen to encounter the supernatural travail, yield to it because you don't know what will be born through that. "The boundary lines have fallen for me in pleasant places; surely I have a delightful inheritance" (Psalm 16:6 NIV).

He has ordained a place for you to operate from with your supply of the Spirit. Stay within that and remember how effective you are. If God has given us the easy way, we won't get any brownie points for doing it the hard way. Keep it simple and keep short accounts with God. Joy will give you the strength to bring forth. An Old Testament Scripture talks about how the people couldn't bring forth. They didn't have enough strength, but with joy, you can draw from the wells of salvation (Isaiah 12:3). Keep it simple and enjoy the journey.

The Spirit is saying,

"I am the Lord, strong and mighty. I have you in the palm of My hand. You are My child, but I have also made you My ambassador. Allow My Spirit to flood your spirit with revelation of My kingdom. You have dominion over the adversary, so take your stand in the Spirit."

~Kevin Zadai

PRAYER:

Father, we pray for all our friends, Lord, that You would give them that spirit of wisdom and revelation in the knowledge of You and that You would strengthen them with might and power in their inner man. Lord, make their path clear before them that they would know to go to the left or to the right. We declare over them that they hear Your voice and the voice of a stranger they do not follow. Lord, heal them of anything that needs to be healed inside, outside, or otherwise. Lord, we thank You for a quick work in their lives, that You would multiply back to them the seeds that they have sown, and that You would encourage them, Lord. May they receive individual encouragement or from a letter or a prophecy You've given them before or even from a song. Strengthen them. We speak joy over them and strength to finish the race. In Jesus's name. Amen.

What did the Holy Spirit reveal to you regarding this chapter?

_____

_____

_____

_____

_____

_____

_____

_____

_____

_____

_____

_____

_____

10

It's God's Plan That Stands

Now faith is the substance of things hoped for,
the evidence of things not seen.
—Hebrews 11:1

When I was a little girl growing up, I had horses. One day, while clearing out the horse pasture, the Lord told me that I would be a Christian and I would always be married. I was not a Christian at that time, and I became less and less of a Christian as I grew older. I went further and further in the wrong direction for many years.

I wasn't born again until my senior year in high school. I was saved because of His goodness. In the back of my mind, I always knew I would be a Christian. To me, it meant that I would straighten out my life and become good enough, and then I'd be a Christian.

That train of thought enabled me to go further down the wrong path because I was looking to myself to do what only Jesus could do. Do you know how far *you* can take yourself? Not that far. You can achieve a few things on your own, but they won't be of any eternal value.

When my mom would go to get her hair done, she would take me, and Toni would do my hair. She was a beautiful younger woman with a family, and her parents owned the salon. I could tell she knew where I was at and what I was up to, but I don't think my mom knew the crowd I was running with was as bad as they were. My mom had grown up in a more sheltered environment in the East with fancy boarding schools, so she didn't have the exposure to the public schools that I did. Toni asked me questions, and she knew what I was doing. One day, she told me how wild she used to be. I thought, *This just does not compute. There's no way she could've ever been wild because she is so sweet, pretty, and healthy-looking.* She was working on my hair, and I asked, "How did you ever change?"

She said, "Oh, I didn't change. I asked Jesus into my heart, and He changed me."

I was shocked; I don't even know that she realized what she did for me. She asked Jesus into her heart, and He changed her! That was the key I needed. A short time later, I came home one night, probably from a party. I went into my room downstairs, and I got down on my knees by my bed, and I just said, "Help. My life's going in the wrong direction. Help me." It wasn't a fancy prayer, but it was a surrender.

The following day, I woke up, and I went upstairs for breakfast with my Bible. My mom knew something was different, and I haven't stopped reading my Bible ever since. All sorts of activities I was involved in just left me. It is the Lord's goodness that leads us to repentance (Romans 2:4). It's not about our circumstances or how impossible our situation is or what problems we may think we have. What leads us to repentance is His goodness. I was mixed up with the wrong person in my first marriage because I thought that everyone changed as much as I had when they received Christ. I found out that you must continue in your relationship with Him. The Lord wants you to keep moving forward and to always give Him your yes.

The Lord told me I would be married, and that thought was always in the background but not necessarily in the forefront. The day after I entered the mission field, that word moved to the forefront. I knew that I was entering that season in life where I would be getting married, and the Lord was highlighting it to me. We can do many things that God is highlighting, but we can also get ahead of Him. You want to get to the point where you could live without His promise and still be okay. You get so far into the victory that you could live without it.

That Sunday when I met Kevin, the anointing came in right before he arrived with our mutual friend Dottie. That's when the Lord asked me, "What are you going to do about what I promised you?" I then realized that I wasn't in faith anymore. He healed and delivered me to the point that I was happy living with the pastor's family, riding horses, and going to church. I was just sort of coasting. When I reflected on my situation, I almost instantly got back into faith, and as I mentioned, the faith began with believing for my former husband to be restored to the Lord, regardless of what anyone thought. That's when Dottie came to introduce me to Kevin. It was as if the Lord took the faith I had, and He saw that I feared Him more than I feared man, and then Kevin was there.

God wanted my faith. He loves it when He sees that you don't care about what other people think as much as you care about Him. You can't set situations up for yourself. We can say all day long, "I choose you, Lord. I'm going to do this instead of that because I love you." But He ordains certain supernatural setups, such as what happened with Abraham and Isaac. We are now living in the faith that Abraham exhibited that day. That was part of the equation for God to offer up Jesus. He chose to connect Himself with His people, and you are connected to God. You are so special to Him. You were created in Him before the foundations of the world. Even though I went through a rough spot before I met Kevin, he was always God's original plan for me.

When you go out and buy something that you love—like a camera, a car, or a toy—and something happens to it or it falls in the mud and gets dirty, that doesn't change its original purpose. You don't leave it dirty; you clean it. The mud is so insignificant compared to the original purpose of that item because God's plan still stands.

The Spirit is saying,

"I have been with you in your mother's womb since your conception. I have written about you before you were you. Trust in Me to bring it to pass. I am well able!"

~Kevin Zadai

PRAYER:

Father, we thank You for the one reading this today. Whatever good work they are created in You for, we come in agreement that it will be fulfilled and that Your victorious voice will reign over their lives and they will be set free to worship You. They will have the freedom to serve You, to glorify You, and to live in You. They will live and breathe in You and have their being. Bless them abundantly and give them strength as they go about their day today. In Jesus's name. Amen.

What did the Holy Spirit reveal to you regarding this chapter?

_____

_____

_____

_____

_____

_____

_____

_____

_____

_____

_____

_____

_____

_____

_____

_____

_____

_____

11

Rest and Trust in Him

This is what the Lord says: "Stand at the crossroads and look; ask for the ancient paths, ask where the good way is, and walk in it, and you will find rest for your souls. But you said, 'We will not walk in it.'
—Jeremiah 6:16 NIV

*T*here is an ancient foundation, an original plan that God had when He created you. On that path, when we're walking in His ways, there is rest. When the Lord put Kevin and me together, we found rest. We can always return to the fact that He brought us together and it was His idea. There is a rest in that, and then we work from that resting place.

There's strength in entering the rest. The Apostle Paul went from killing Christians to helping probably more Christians than most people have next to Jesus. His original purpose was to be an apostle. His purpose was to bring the revelation of Jesus Christ into this realm that was not here before. He wrote a big chunk of the New Testament. After Jesus accomplished His work, those revelations were released. God's original purpose for your life is more real than any circumstance that you are facing.

Kevin always felt like he would meet me at Rhema, the Bible College he attended, but he left Rhema without meeting his wife. I had it on my heart to go to Rhema but ended up going to YWAM. We both love Rhema and were so thankful for Brother Hagin, and we still listen to him all the time. God brought Kevin and me together; it was His original purpose for us.

Brian McCallum gave us a prophetic word from Jesus. He used to fly a Blackbird, the SR-71 spy plane. Brian was an astronaut and lieutenant colonel who flew at the edge of space. He was asked to become part of the space program as the first space shuttle pilot, but he left it all to follow the Lord. The Lord told Brian that he would be the pilot for Kenneth Hagin Sr, so that's what he went and did. He left the opportunity as the first space pilot and obeyed the call of the Lord to serve and be in the ministry. His obedience was so important to us and so many others whose lives were impacted by him. He helped thousands of people besides us, but he was in the right place, all because he obeyed the Lord.

Kevin decided to visit Brian, who had become the dean of students at Rhema. Kevin wanted to ask him why he hadn't met his wife at Rhema even though he felt he should have. Kevin said he had felt as if something had died. He was sitting there in front of Brian at his desk, and he asked him, "What do you think happened?" Brian's initial reaction was that he did not know and did not have a witness from the Holy Spirit regarding Kevin's question.

At the time, Kevin had been working for a year as a volunteer within the ministry before Southwest Airlines hired him. Right when Brian responded and said, "I don't know," the power of God hit him and came into the room of his office. Kevin said he never saw Brian become that emotional, but Brian fell face down on his desk and couldn't get up. He was shaking and crying, and he said, "Jesus is behind me with His hands on my shoulders, and He wants me to tell you that it's not your fault that you didn't meet her here because she took a different path, and it will take her four years to get back on track. If she does and if she's obedient, then you will meet her in four years. If not, I will groom someone else for you, and

I will have them take her place." Then Jesus walked out of the room, and Brian got up and said, "What just happened?" He couldn't explain what had happened; Jesus completely took over.

I was so humbled to know that Brian had given us the word of the Lord. When that word was given, Kevin was in Tulsa, and I was in Seattle about to enter a wrong marriage, but God was already speaking. It's comforting to know that God already knew, and He was involved in our lives. There's just so much great news, and He is such a good God. I had entered my previous marriage in 1989, and it took me four years to heal. I was in such a rough spot, but I managed to get back on track by the grace of God. In January 1993, I met Kevin. We got married in May 1993, exactly four years later.

I think of that Scripture that says, at the right time, when we were still powerless, Christ died for us (Romans 5:6 NIV). That was my story of salvation. I was powerless. He died for me on my worst day, not on my best day. It always strengthens me to know that it's not me. The same thing happened with our marriage; it was by grace. We can do everything we know to do, but it's by His grace through faith that we can do anything (Ephesians 2:8–9). You can take comfort in knowing it's not you. We don't look to ourselves and boast. No matter what we think we know or how many years we've been in the Lord, it's still by grace through faith. We can't boast.

I can't boast that I got back on track. I'm just thankful I did. It wasn't a big sin that kept me away; it was more that I felt so vulnerable, and I didn't know what to do. I thank God for my pastors who took me in. They had been through a rough spot in their marriage at one point, and they recovered, and I thought, *There's no way. Their marriage survived, and these people are so in love with each other*. It's as though God put them in front of me just to show me that you could live through being heartbroken.

Whatever you believe Him for, whether it's a marriage or something else, He will bring you to a place where you're so happy. Whether it happens or not, you're still okay. He wants you to be where the Word of God is complete in you. Faith is the substance of things hoped for, the evidence of things not seen (Hebrews 11:1). I knew this verse and often read it, but that day at the dock, when God brought it to me, I understood it for myself. I had gotten it, and I had faith. Suddenly, I had faith through worshipping, following Him, having the right people in my life, and spending time in the Word. I knew I had the faith to be married.

When the Lord asked me, "What are you going to do about what I promised you?" I was shocked because I was trying to make sure that what happened in that other marriage never happened again. When you reach that place, you have so much joy, which is how we're created to live. We are the King's kids, and we shouldn't have a worry or care in the world because it's all been taken care of. We were already created in Him. He knew you before you were born and even before your parents were born. We were created in Him for good works before Adam and Eve were born.

You were already destined for greatness. That truth should cause you to feel like you just went to a spiritual chiropractor, where everything inside you has come into alignment and there is nothing but joy and rest. That's what we have in Him, and we must stop trying to get what we already have. That's what happened to Adam and Eve. They had everything they needed, and the devil was trying to get them to receive what they already had. He tried to tempt Jesus in the desert, and he challenged Him, "*If* you're the Son of God." God just finished telling Jesus He *was* the Son of God.

Obviously, the devil wasn't listening. The Spirit of God descended on Jesus and said, "This is my beloved Son in whom I am well pleased." Then a few pages later, the devil said, "If you're the Son of God." He was trying to get Jesus to doubt who He was. One of the biggest things to watch out for is the devil trying to get you to be someone you already are.

The Spirit is saying,

"It is time to fall back into My arms and let Me hold you. There is nothing that My love will not do for you if you will simply rest in Me."

~Kevin Zadai

PRAYER:

Lord, we declare that the identity of Your child would be restored to Jesus today. We agree that their hearts are made whole and that they would know who they are in You. May they come to know everything You spoke in Your Word is a testament to their lives and their hearts today. May they receive and treasure Your love within them above anything else. Lord, because they trust in You, their eyes are set on You, no matter what is happening in their lives. Thank You, Lord, for total victory, total deliverance, and total joy in their lives. In Jesus's name. Amen.

What did the Holy Spirit reveal to you regarding this chapter?

_____

_____

_____

_____

_____

_____

_____

_____

_____

_____

_____

_____

_____

_____

_____

_____

_____

12

God's Original Purpose

But the plans of the Lord stand firm forever, the
purposes of His heart through all generations.
—Psalm 33:11

$\mathcal{G}$od prepared me for Kevin, and when we met,
he said he knew I was the one God had for him.
Kevin tells our story like this:

In August '92, I went in for surgery and
encountered Jesus in heaven. When I was
there, I didn't think about marriage, and it
didn't bother me that I hadn't been married
on earth. In heaven, you're married to Jesus.
You have no conscious thoughts about the
opposite sex because we're all family. We are
like the angels.

When Jesus sent me back and put me in my
body, I was so immersed in the glory of God

that I couldn't do much. I laid in bed for about three weeks. It took my body several years to fully recover, but my spirit was alive.

I began to study the Scriptures more. I worked at my job and was a singer in the music ministry at church. One night while I was on my way home after practice, I pulled into the driveway where I was staying, and it felt as if someone got into my car and sat down beside me. It was only a few weeks after the operation, and the Lord had told me that something would happen very soon and that I was supposed to get ready. The presence stayed in the car for a while, and then I felt as if they left the car.

The glory went with me into the house. I was staying with an elderly woman named Dottie in a room in her house while I traveled with the airline. When I came into the house, Dottie looked at me and said, "What just happened to you? The glory of God is on you?"

I replied, "I just had a visitation, and it was either an angel or Jesus— I didn't see who it was, but they told me I would go to Seattle this weekend and that I would meet my wife."

Dottie said, "Well, I'm going to Seattle this weekend, and I already know who your wife is." She started laughing, and the glory became so intense that we both collapsed under the power of God. We ended up laughing on the floor for a long time.

The time came the following week, and Dottie flew up there and called me, and she said, "You know, I'm not going to tell you who your wife is, but I've known for about a year. I'm just going to introduce you to a bunch of people, and I'll let the Lord tell you who it is." I flew up there, and Dottie picked me up at the airport, and we stayed at her daughter's house. On Sunday morning, she took us to church.

I walked into the church and saw Kathi sitting on the second row, and the Lord said, "That's your wife."

Ever since I was saved at nineteen years old, I would go under the stars each night and pray for my wife because I knew that she was alive somewhere and would be out under those same stars. I did that by faith for all those years until the day came that He told me to go to Seattle. It was a big step of faith to travel thirteen hundred miles to a city I had never been to in order to meet my wife.

I canceled a bunch of responsibilities I had with the ministry. I was going to be singing for an evangelist with Israel Houghton. I told Israel that I couldn't come, and he just laughed when I called him back and told him that I met her. I made plans to come back up a second time to see Kathi. Our relationship progressed from there. We were married in four months. Twenty-eight years later, we are so very happy that God synchronized our life so strategically so we could be together.

After I met Kevin and before he came up the second time, I started to see his face. I would be working at my shop in Woodinville, Washington, doing hair, and I'd see his smiling face sometimes. I thought it was odd because I was so focused on walking out that other marriage.

Someone once sent me flowers at work, and I thought, *It's either who I was married to before, or maybe Kevin sent them. But wait, why would I think they could be from Kevin?* It turned out to be a thank you from a lady I sowed my wedding dress to. Around that time, I felt like I was supposed to sow my wedding dress to a bridal shop, and I told the Christian lady who owned the shop that if anyone came in and couldn't afford a dress, to sow it to them. The woman who received the dress sent me the flowers.

Kevin decided to come back a second time, and he stayed with the assistant pastors from our church. He came over to the house, and we all had pizza, and he watched us go horseback riding. My pastors knew Kevin was the one as well. I was a little bit slow, but I got the revelation after Kevin left. The night he left, we all put the horses away. They left a little bit early because it was freezing, and they weren't appropriately dressed. Kevin had a nice leather coat on, but it was still too cold outside. We all hugged goodbye, just like you do at any Christian gathering, and I hugged Kevin, but I didn't think anything of it until I got home.

I felt led to pull out the prophecy God gave me about how He would restore me in the area of marriage. When I read it, He said, "I'll again place you in the arms of another man." I had not focused on that part of the prophecy until that night. I had put my focus on getting out of the other marriage, seeking direction, and being restored. When I read that part of the prophecy, I had the realization, and the light came on. I thought, *Oh my goodness, Kevin is the person God was talking about in the prophecy. He said, "I will place you in the arms of another man, and you will know him by his commitment and the words he speaks."* It was Kevin who God had for me, and I just realized it that day.

We had our first date, and Kevin took me to the Space Needle. When we were there, a presence of peace came in, and Kevin told me how much he loved me. I had never enjoyed hearing those words because it usually wasn't the case, but when Kevin was telling me, I sensed that the Lord was standing there, and He said, "See, I told you." There was so much peace.

When I got home, the pastors and their kids were waiting for me; they were excited. They asked, "What do you think?" At first, I didn't have an answer, then suddenly I did—the peace. There was so much peace when we were together; it was another level of peace.

If you're considering the next step in your life, whether it's marriage or something else, if it's not taking you into more peace, then you don't want it. You don't want to go backward. He's taking us from glory to glory. (See 2 Corinthians 3:18.) Kevin's unspoken prayer request was that he wanted to get married on his birthday, and God arranged it so that we were married on his birthday. Many supernatural events led up to that day. We encountered Jesus while at a restaurant in Washington. I went to order for us, and Kevin went into the restroom. He said that the wall in the bathroom disappeared, and Jesus started to talk to him about getting married. He gave Kevin instructions, and then He disappeared.

We got married that weekend in a town called Selah in eastern Washington. What's interesting is David would write the word *selah* after a couple of verses in the Psalms. In Hebrew, it means to stop, meditate, and calmly think.[3] God put so many details together and confirmed them for us, and we were a total miracle. There is no way we could have found each other in the whole world, but God made it possible because it was His original plan and purpose.

---

[3] "Selah," Bible Study Tools, accessed September 30, 2021, https://www.biblestudytools.com/dictionary/selah.

The Spirit is saying,

"I, the Lord, am over the times and the seasons of My kingdom in heaven and earth. I will work with those who desire to pray My perfect will to come into this realm called earth. I uphold the absolute truth of My throne. Command it to come to you now. You are My ambassadors!"

~Kevin Zadai

PRAYER:

Thank You, Lord, for Your blood covenant that You made with each person reading this. The precious blood of Jesus is stronger than any circumstance they might be facing right now. We thank You for Your victory in their lives and how You have delivered them. I impart hope to them in the name of Jesus and pray that they would encounter wisdom, peace, and joy as they go into their destiny, Lord. Thank You for what is to come. You will bring clarity when they make decisions, and Lord, they have nothing to fear in Jesus's name. Amen.

What did the Holy Spirit reveal to you regarding this chapter?

_____

_____

_____

_____

_____

_____

_____

_____

_____

_____

_____

_____

_____

_____

_____

_____

_____

_____

_____

Salvation Prayer

Lord God,
I confess that I am a sinner.
I confess that I need Your Son, Jesus.
Please forgive me in His name.
Lord Jesus, I believe You died for me and that
You are alive and listening to me now.
I now turn from my sins and welcome You into my heart.
Come and take control of my life.
Make me the kind of person You want me to be.
Now, fill me with Your Holy Spirit, who will show me
how to live for You. I acknowledge You before men as
my Savior and my Lord. In Jesus's name. Amen.

If you prayed this prayer, please contact us at
info@kevinzadai.com for more information and
materials.

We welcome you to join our network at Warriornotes.tv
for access to exclusive programming.

To enroll in our ministry school, go to:
www.Warriornotesschool.com.

Visit KevinZadai.com for additional
ministry materials.

About Dr. Kevin L. Zadai

Kevin Zadai, ThD, was called to the ministry at the age of ten. He attended Central Bible College in Springfield, Missouri, where he received a bachelor of arts in theology. Later, he received training in missions at Rhema Bible College and a ThD at Primus University. He is currently ordained through Rev. Dr. Jesse and Rev. Dr. Cathy Duplantis.

At the age of thirty-one, during a routine day surgery, he found himself "on the other side of the veil" with Jesus. For forty-five minutes, the Master revealed spiritual truths before returning him to his body and assigning him to a supernatural ministry.

Kevin holds a commercial pilot's license and is retired from Southwest Airlines after twenty-nine years as a flight attendant. Kevin is the founder and president of Warrior Notes School of Ministry. He and his lovely wife, Kathi, reside in New Orleans, Louisiana.

Other Books and Study Guides by Dr. Kevin L. Zadai

Kevin has written over fifty books and study guides Please see our website at www.Kevinzadai.com for a complete list of materials!

60-Day Healing Devotional

A Meeting Place with God, The Heavenly Encounters Series Volume 1

The Heavenly Encounters Series Volume 1

The Agenda of Angels

The Agenda of Angels Study Guide

Days of Heaven on Earth

Days of Heaven on Earth: A Study Guide to the Days Ahead

Days of Heaven on Earth Prayer and Confession Guide

Encountering the Heavenly Sapphire Devotional

Encountering the Heavenly Sapphire Study Guide

Encountering God's Normal

Encountering God's Will

Encountering God's Normal

Encountering God's Normal Study Guide

From Breakthrough to Overthrow Study Guide

Have you Been to the Altar Lately?